Marian Catechist Manual

By John A. Hardon, S.J.

ISBN: 1-931101-00-0

Marian Catechist Manual

Imprimatur:
†Most Reverend Raymond L. Burke, D.D., J.C.D.
Bishop of La Crosse
July 14, 2000

Published and distributed with
the permission of Inter Mirifica by
ETERNAL LIFE
P.O. Box 787
Bardstown, Kentucky 40004

ISBN 1-931101-00-0

90000>

9 781931 101004

Contents

Anima Christi ix

Preface xi

Introduction xv

Index of Abbreviations xix

Purpose 1

Motto 1

Members 2

Formation 4

Spiritual Practices 6

Candidacy and
Pre-Commitment Formation 7

Commitment 9

Marian Catechist Apostolate 9

Contributed Services 12

Transmitting Christ's Teaching 14

Lifelong Formation 16

Study of the Word of God 16

Familiarity with God 17

Spirit of Prayer 18

Self-Detachment 19

The Active and
   Contemplative Apostolates 21

The Holy Eucharist 22

Threefold Sacrament 23

Grace through the Humanity of Christ .. 26

Mary, the Model Catechist 30

The Faith of Mary 32

The Faith of Marian Catechists 35

The Prayer of Mary 36

The Prayer of a Marian Catechist 38

The Life of Mary.................... 43

The Life of a Marian Catechist 46

The Vicar of Christ 47

Papal Primacy 48

Practical Implications 51

Scope of the Marian Catechist
   Apostolate 56

   Infants 56

Children 58

Adolescents. 59

Young Adults 61

Adults. 62

Ways and Means to Be Used
    by Marian Catechists 67

Family Catechists 69

What Are Parental Rights? 72

Sources of Parental Rights 76

Parental Responsibilities 77

Personal Responsibility 78

Role of the Marian Catechists 83

Conduct of Marian Catechists 87

Marian Associates. 89

Anima Christi

Soul of Christ, sanctify me.
Body of Christ, save me.
Blood of Christ, inebriate me.
Water from the Side of Christ,
wash me;
Passion of Christ, strengthen me.
O good Jesus, hear me.
Within Thy Wounds hide me.
Suffer me not to be separated from Thee.
From the malicious enemy defend me.
In the hour of my death call me
And bid me come to Thee,
That with Thy saints I may praise Thee,
For ever and ever.
Amen.

PREFACE

Some twenty years ago, our Holy Father Pope John Paul II asked Mother Teresa of Calcutta to train her Sisters, the Missionaries of Charity, to be catechists. At the same time, the Holy See asked Father John Hardon, S.J., to organize the catechetical training program for the Missionaries of Charity. The fruit of the catechetical work of the Missionaries of Charity has been extraordinary. Mother Teresa's Sisters are now in over one-hundred countries, teaching the faith and its practice, faithful to their charism of service to Christ in "the poorest of the poor."

One of the special fruits of Father Hardon's work with the Missionaries of Charity has been the foundation of the Marian Catechists to work with the Missionaries of Charity and eventually to carry out the apostolate of evangelization and catechesis throughout the world. He has founded and developed the association of Marian Catechists in faithful service to the See of Peter, in accord with the original request of his help in the spiritual and doctrinal formation of catechists.

Marian Catechists devote themselves to growth in their own spiritual life and in their knowledge and practice of the Catholic faith, so that they may hand on the Catholic faith and its practice to others. As more and more catechists have learned of the Marian Catechists, they have joined them in order to fortify themselves spiritually and doctrinally for the challenging apostolate of catechesis in our time. The Marian Catechists now have members in some twenty-five dioceses in the United States.

The *Marian Catechist Manual* is the fruit of twenty years of tireless work to form catechists both spiritually and doctrinally. It sets forth the noble goals of the Marian Catechists and the means by which those goals are to be achieved. For the Marian Catechists, it is the guidebook which helps them to develop spiritually and doctrinally for the mission of catechesis, which is at the foundation of the life of the Church. For all catechists, it provides inspiration and direction for their important service to the Church. God willing, it will lead many catechists follow the way of the Marian Catechists and so to find lifelong spiritual and doctrinal formation in carrying out the apostolate of catechesis.

The *Marian Catechists Manual* is now published by Father John A. Hardon, S.J., to the greater glory of God and for the salvation of souls.

Most Reverend Raymond L. Burke
Bishop of La Crosse

INTRODUCTION

We live in the most highly educated nation in world history. But, except for a small remnant, most Americans are abysmally ignorant of God's laws and His promises.

In 1972 Pope Paul VI said, "Satan's smoke has made its way into the temple of God..." Now, as we enter the third millennium, it is no longer "smoke" but a raging fire. Catholicism is in the throes of the worst crisis in its entire history. Unless true and loyal Catholics have the zeal and the spirit of the early Christians, unless they are willing to do what they did and to pay the price that they paid, the days of America are numbered.

God knows the past, present and future. He put us here at this time and place knowing full well the gravity of our times. His grace is available in superabundance. How can this infinite storehouse of graces be tapped?

The early Christians attended Mass and received Holy Communion daily. This gave them heroic fortitude and courage to evangelize in the face of martyrdom. They "went to school" in the catacombs to gain the knowledge and build the cunning and the zeal to win souls for Christ.

Today's Catholics should also attend Mass and receive Holy Communion daily, if possible. They should "go to school" in their home or in their car, to instill knowledge and strength of will to evangelize. But with the eternal destiny of millions in the balance, still more is needed - an elite, heroic and zealous Catholic movement.

The Marian Catechist Apostolate is organized and ready to train thousands countrywide. Its sights are set on restoring, revitalizing, reforming and converting millions.

THE MARIAN CATECHIST must have the zeal and desire to be a part of this brilliant renaissance – of a new way of life dedicated to filling the massive void caused by formerly faithful religious nuns and brothers who have abandoned their teaching vocation by the tens of thousands.

As you read through this manual, keep in mind the need for catechists. Pray for the grace to be a part of this great movement. There is no requirement to leave your profession, quit your job, or move to a new location.

The early Christians succeeded; the Marian Catechist can, too!

Father John A. Hardon, S.J.
Founder and Spiritual Director

INDEX OF ABBREVIATIONS USED IN THE TEXT

ChL	*Christifideles Laici*
GDC	General Directory for Catechesis
CCC	Catechism of the Catholic Church
CIC	*Codex Iuris Canonici*
CT	*Catechesi Tradendae*
RH	*Redemptor Hominis*
EN	*Evangelii Nuntiandi*
IM	*Inter Mirifica*

Purpose

1. The purpose of the Marian Catechists is twofold:

- To cultivate a deep devotion to the Holy Eucharist and the Blessed Virgin Mary, and a special loyalty to the Vicar of Christ, the Bishop of Rome.

- To teach the Catholic religion, personally and through the media of social communication, especially to Catholic families throughout the world.

Motto

2. Marian Catechists will have as their motto the words of the Blessed Virgin Mary to the servants at the wedding feast at Cana: "Do whatever He tells you" (John 2:5). It was after this directive of His Blessed Mother that Our Lord used

the work of these servants to perform His first miracle.

Members

3. Members of the Marian Catechists are adult Catholic lay people, whether single, married, or widowed. (Cf. John Paul II, Post-synodal Apostolic Exhortation, *Christifideles Laici [ChL]*, 30 December 1988, 9)

In order to qualify as Marian Catechists, they must be (Cf. *ChL, 30)*

- firm believers in the Catholic faith, as expressed in the *Catechism of the Catholic Church;*

- adequately educated to be effective communicators of the Gospel, revealed by Jesus Christ and entrusted to the Church He founded on the Apostles under the authority of Peter and his successors in the papacy (Cf. Sacred

Congregation for the Clergy, *General Directory for Catechesis [GDC]*, 11 August 1997, 235);

- strongly motivated to share with others the true faith which they possess;

- sufficiently free to devote some time every week to working in the apostolate of the Marian Catechists;

- willing to follow such directives as are given for the cooperative efforts of the Marian Catechists.

There are two forms of membership in the Marian Catechists: the actively apostolic and the spiritually contemplative.

- The actively apostolic members are engaged in the corporate catechetical work of the Marian Catechists.

- The spiritually contemplative dedicate their prayers, sacrifices and sufferings to obtain God's blessing on the

Church, on Bishops and priests, on the work of promoting the faith, and especially on the Marian Catechists' apostolate.

FORMATION

4. There are three stages in the formation of the Marian Catechists. (Cf. *ChL 63*)

    a) The first stage. After admission to the program, the candidate agrees to perform certain acts of piety, daily, weekly or monthly, as expected of the candidates. He or she is also to make the Spiritual Exercises of St. Ignatius, privately, for thirty days, during the candidacy period. The candidate also agrees to complete the 16-lesson Basic Catholic Catechist's Home-Study Course based on the *Catechism of the Catholic Church*. (Cf. *GDC 261*)

b) The second stage lasts one year. During this time, the participants are to complete the more advanced 36-lesson Catholic Catechist's Home-Study Course as well as fulfill the required practices of piety. They also engage in some catechetical activity, depending on their eventual commitment as Marian Catechists.

c) The third stage is a continuing process on three levels of commitment, namely spiritual, doctrinal and catechetical, as follows:

- Commitment by a Marian Catechist to observe certain basic norms of the spiritual life;

- Commitment by a Marian Catechist to deepen his or her understanding of the Catholic faith, as contained in the *Catechism of the Catholic Church,* Sacred

Scripture and Tradition, and as taught by the Church's Magisterium under the Vicar of Christ;

- Commitment to cooperate with other Marian Catechists in disseminating the revealed truths to others according to the catechetical and pedagogical principles and norms set forth in the *General Directory for Catechesis*.

This third stage of commitment is called lifetime formation because a Marian Catechist can give others only what he or she has. In His ordinary providence, God uses human instruments as channels of His blessing according to the measure of their own union with Him and the possession of His grace.

SPIRITUAL PRACTICES

5. The spiritual practices of the Marian Catechists depend on two factors: their stage of formation, and their eventual

degree of commitment to the Marian Catechist apostolate.

Candidacy and Pre-Commitment Formation

6. On this level, the spiritual practices of the Marian Catechists are a development process.

Those in the Candidacy Program are to adopt gradually the following spiritual practices:

- Mass and Holy Communion at least three times a week;

- Daily recitation of five decades of the Rosary;

- Recitation of the Angelus at least twice each day;

- Reception of the Sacrament of Confession at least once a month;

- Recitation of the Morning Offering of the Apostleship of Prayer in the morning;

- A five-minute examination of conscience each evening before retiring;

- Spiritual reading for at least ten minutes each day;

- Daily meditation for at least ten minutes, which may be prayerful reflection on the spiritual reading. For those in the Pre-Commitment Formation the practices are the same as for those in the Candidacy Formation, except that the following practices become habitual:

- Mass and Holy Communion should be daily;

- Reception of the Sacrament of Confession or Penance should be at least twice a month;

- The spiritual reading and meditation (or meditative reading) should be at least fifteen minutes each day;

- The Way of the Cross is to be made daily.

Commitment

7. For those who have made their commitment as Marian Catechists, the spiritual practices are the same as in the Pre-Commitment Formation. The basic difference is that a formal commitment has been made to follow these practices faithfully.

Marian Catechist Apostolate

8. The heart of the Marian Catechist Apostolate is to fulfill Christ's directive to proclaim the Gospel to all nations, teaching them to observe everything which He had commanded His disciples. (Cf. *Cat-*

echism of the Catholic Church [CCC], 11 October 1992, 849)

Marian Catechists, therefore, are to engage in extending the Kingdom of Christ here on earth, in order to extend His dominion over the hearts of men in the kingdom of heaven for all eternity. (Cf. *Codex Iuris Canonici [CIC], 25 January 1983,* Canon 225)

In carrying out their apostolate, Marian Catechists take their inspiration from the Savior's declaration in His prayer to the Father at the Last Supper, "And this is eternal life, that they know thee the only true God, and Jesus Christ whom thou hast sent." (John 13:3)

The key work in the apostolate of the Marian Catechists is to make God known through Christ so that knowing God, people might love Him, and loving Him might serve Him, and serving Him might save their souls.

As explained by Pope John Paul II, everything else than Jesus Christ is secondary. "The primary and essential object of catechesis", writes the Holy Father, "is. . . the mystery of Christ." The main purpose of catechizing is very simple:

> It is to *reveal* in the Person of Christ the whole of God's eternal design reaching fulfillment in that Person. It is to seek to *understand* the meaning of Christ's actions and words and of the signs worked by Him, for they simultaneously hide and reveal His mystery. Accordingly, the definitive aim of catechesis is to put people not only in touch but in communion, in intimacy, with Jesus Christ: only He can lead us to the love of the Father in the Spirit and make us share in the life of the Holy Trinity. (John Paul II, Apostolic

Exhortation, *Catechesi Tradendae*
[CT], 16 October 1979, 5)

This stress on making God known in the Person of Christ is not coincidental. It is of the essence of Christianity. Why? Because, "faith then depends on hearing, and hearing on the word of Christ." (Romans 10:17) Those who believe in Christ must witness to their faith in Christ, so that others might hear and see the faith professed and thus be led to believe (or deepen their belief) in Jesus Christ.

Marian Catechists are to be living witnesses to their faith in Christ and thus become channels of believing grace to other people.

Contributed Services

9. The basic work of the Marian Catechist Apostolate is to be done by dedicated persons without financial remuneration.

This is consistent with the whole history of the apostolic work of the Catholic Church. All the great achievements of evangelization have been done by individuals, through corporate enterprises, in keeping with Christ's directives to His first disciples. He commanded the Twelve and began to send them forth two by two; and He gave them power over the unclean spirits. He instructed them to take nothing for their journey, but a staff only — no wallet, no bread, no money in their girdle, but to wear sandals, and not to put on two tunics. And He said to them, "Wherever you enter into a house, stay there until you leave the place." (Mk. 6:7-10) The core of the Church's proclamation of the Good News has been such selfless love of Christ that apostles of the Word have labored, not for money, but out of love for the Savior in the extension of His Kingdom. The heart of the Marian Catechist Apostolate must be the selfless dedication of men and women who are willing to follow the poor Christ in the proclamation of His revealed truth.

TRANSMITTING CHRIST'S TEACHING

10. No less important than sharing their own faith with others is the duty of Marian Catechists to remain faithful in transmitting only Christ's teaching, and not their own or other people's ideas. (Cf. *CIC* 227)

Whatever be the level of his responsibility in the Church, every catechist must constantly endeavor to transmit by his teaching and behavior the teaching and life of Jesus. He will not seek to keep directed towards himself and his personal opinions and attitudes the attention and the consent of the mind and heart of the person he is catechizing. Above all, he will not try to inculcate his personal opinions and options as if they expressed Christ's teaching and the lessons of His life. Every catechist should be able to apply to himself the mysterious words of Jesus: "My teaching is not mine, but His who sent me." St. Paul did this when he was dealing with a question of prime importance: "I received from the Lord what I also delivered to you." (*CT* 6)

In the light of this fidelity to Christ's teaching, Marian Catechists must preserve that rare combination of having a mind of their own indeed, but a mind that is humbly obedient to the mind of Christ.

It is not rhetoric, therefore, but hard reality to require four qualities of every Marian Catechist. In the words of Pope John Paul II:

- "What assiduous study of the word of God transmitted by the Church's Magisterium,

- "What profound familiarity with Christ and the Father,

- "What a spirit of prayer,

- "What detachment from self must a catechist have in order that he may say 'My teaching is not mine.'" (*CT* 6)

LIFELONG FORMATION

11. Marian Catechists need a lifelong formation in the four qualities expected of everyone who wants to be a true catechist.

STUDY OF THE WORD OF GOD

12. In its basic meaning, study is not so much an academic discipline as a zealous acquisition of knowledge in order to share one's learning with other persons.

To study, therefore, means to learn so that

I may pass on to other minds whatever knowledge I have personally acquired. The knowledge that a Marian Catechist should acquire is the knowledge of Catholic faith and morality, liturgy and spirituality, canon law and Church history. All of these are to be learned according to the Church's Magisterium, that is, her teaching authority as vested in the successors of the Apostles under the primacy of the successor of Peter, the Bishop of Rome.

In accord with the directives of the Apostolic See, Marian Catechists employ a twofold vademecum in their apostolate: the *Catechism of the Catholic Church* for doctrine and the *General Directory for Catechesis* for catechetical method (*Cf. GDC 8, 9*).

FAMILIARITY WITH GOD

13. The knowledge of a Marian Catechist must not be sterile information but a fruit-

ful wisdom that becomes living knowledge which produces good fruits in a life that responds with generosity to the inspirations of the Holy Spirit. (Cf. *GDC 156)*

Implied in this generous response to God's grace is more than just giving others a good example. It is certainly deeper than merely not contradicting by his or her conduct what the Marian Catechist teaches by his or her words. It is nothing less than allowing Christ to teach through the catechist, by blessing his or her words with an apostolic fecundity that only a holy life can hope to achieve. (Cf. *GDC* 142)

SPIRIT OF PRAYER

14. The Marian Catechist is not only faithful to the required exercises of piety. He or she is a person who sincerely strives to live in the spirit of prayer. The Marian Cat-

echist cultivates the habit of living in the presence of God. (Cf. *CCC 2565*)

How does this living in the divine presence differ from the practice of familiarity with God? It differs as action differs from disposition or as actual correspondence with God's grace differs from the constant readiness to do His will.

Self-Detachment

15. Underlying the previous three qualities of a good catechist is internal detachment from creatures. (Cf. *CCC 2544*)

Since the spirituality of the Marian Catechist is based on that of St. Ignatius Loyola, it will be useful to quote some of his maxims on detachment and self-conquest.

• We should make more account of renouncing self-will than of raising others from the dead.

- Each person should convince himself that he will make progress in the spiritual life in proportion to his detachment from self and the desire for personal advantage.

- The empty honors of earth cannot satisfy you. Your heart is not narrow enough for the whole world to suffice for it. Nothing but God can fill it. I am not trying to extinguish your ardor for glory, nor inspire you with mean thoughts. Be ambitious, be high-minded, but let your ambition aim higher by despising all that is perishable.

- Life would be unbearable to me if I were to discover in the depths of my soul some remains of what is human and which did not belong entirely to God.

These are the kind of sentiments that a Marian Catechist should ask our Lord to give him or her. They are the seed bed for a fruitful apostolate. (Cf. *CCC 852*)

THE ACTIVE AND CONTEMPLATIVE APOSTOLATES

16. The two forms of membership in the Marian Catechists are not mutually exclusive. Those engaged in the active apostolate need the prayers and sacrifices of the spiritually contemplative, and vice versa. Without the active apostolate, the Marian Catechists would lack the scope and purpose for their existence. Without prayer and sacrifice, Marian Catechists would lack the supernatural means and resources to reach the souls of those who are being catechized. (Cf. *CCC 901*)

Although structurally we may speak of two forms of membership, the two are really inseparable. It is simply that some Marian Catechists are more free to participate in the immediate work of catechesis, while others are more able to offer their interior union with God and self-surrender to His will for the extension of the Kingdom of Christ on earth.

THE HOLY EUCHARIST

17. The center of a Marian Catechist's spiritual life is a deep faith in the Eucharist as Sacrifice of the Mass, Holy Communion, and Real Presence. At the center of this faith is the realization that Jesus Christ, the Son of God, became the Son of Mary to be with us, on earth, as He promised, until the end of time. (Cf. *CCC 1357*)

Marian Catechists must develop this Eucharistic faith if they hope to become apt instruments in the hands of God for the salvation and sanctification of others. It is no coincidence, but deeply providential that the Marian Catechists should have come into existence during the pontificate of Pope John Paul II, the great promoter of devotion to the Holy Eucharist as the triple sacrament of Christ's love. (Cf. *CCC 1324*)

THREEFOLD SACRAMENT

18. Given its cardinal importance, Marian Catechists should grow in their understanding of what the Vicar of Christ means when he says that there is only one Sacrament of the Eucharist and yet this sacrament confers grace in three different ways. Each manner of divine grace corresponds to the three forms in which the Eucharist has been instituted by Christ.

    It is at one and the same time a Sacrifice- Sacrament, a Communion-Sacrament, and a Presence-Sacrament.

(John Paul II, Encyclical Letter, *Redemptor Hominis [RH]*, 4 March 1979, Part IV, 20)

The revealed foundation for this conclusion is the fact of Christ's abiding presence in the Eucharist. It is the "Redeemer of Man" who by His passion and death on the cross merited the grace of our salvation. But it is mainly through the Eucharist that the same Jesus Christ now channels this grace to a sinful human race.

It is in this comprehensive sense that we can say, "The Church lives by the Eucharist, by the fullness of this sacrament." This fullness, however, spans all three levels of its sacramental existence, where, by "sacrament," the Church means a sensible sign, instituted by Christ, through which invisible grace and inward sanctification are communicated to the soul.

The Mass is the Sacrifice-Sacrament of the Eucharist. As the Council of Trent declared "the Sacrifice of the Mass is not only an offering of praise and thanksgiving," it is also a source of grace: "By this oblation, the Lord is appeased, He grants grace and the gift of repentance, and He pardons wrong-doings and sins. The blessings of Redemption which Christ won for us by His bloody death on Calvary are now received in abundance through this unbloody oblation." (Trent, XXII, Ch. II, 9-17-1562)

Holy Communion is the Communion-Sacrament of the Eucharist. As the same Council of Trent defined, Christ present in the Eucharist is not only spiritually eaten, but also really and sacramentally. We actually receive His Body and Blood, and we are truly nourished by His grace. It was Christ's will "that this Sacrament be received as the soul's spiritual food, to sustain and build up those who live with His life."

It is also to be "a remedy to free us from our daily defects and to keep us from mortal sin." (Trent, XIII, Ch. I, 10-11-1551)

The Real Presence is the Presence-Sacrament of the Eucharist. How? The Real Presence is a Sacrament in every way that the humanity of Christ is a channel of grace to those who believe that the Son of God became man for our salvation. (Cf. *CCC 1374*)

GRACE THROUGH THE HUMANITY OF CHRIST

19. The underlying theme of the Church's Eucharistic teaching is the fact of "Christ's consoling presence in the Blessed Sacrament. His real presence in the fullest sense; the substantial presence by which the whole and complete Christ, God and man, is present." (Pope John Paul II, September 29, 1979)

Once this fact of faith is recognized, it is not difficult to see why prayer before the Blessed Sacrament is so efficacious. Indeed it explains why, without a second thought, Catholics have simply referred to the Real Presence as the Blessed *Sacrament*. It is a Sacrament, or better, it is the one Sacrament which not only confers grace but contains the very source of grace, namely Jesus Christ.

As we read the Gospels, we are struck by the marvelous power that Christ's humanity had in effecting changes in the persons who came into contact with Him. Already in the womb of His mother, He sanctified the unborn John the Baptist the moment Elizabeth heard the voice of Mary. At Cana in Galilee, at His mother's request, Jesus told the servants, "Fill the jars with water." When the steward tasted the water, it had turned into wine.

Jesus spoke with human lips when He preached the Sermon on the Mount, when He taught the parables, when He forgave sinners, when He rebuked the Pharisees, when He foretold His Passion and told followers to carry the cross. Jesus touched the blind with human hands, and healed the lepers by speaking with a human voice. On one occasion a sick woman touched the hem of His garment. The woman was instantly healed. Immediately, relates St. Mark, aware that power had gone out from Him, Jesus turned round in the crowd and said, "Who touched my cloak?" Significantly, Jesus told her, "your faith has restored you to health."

All through His public ministry, the humanity of Christ was the means by which He enlightened the minds of His listeners, restored their souls to divine friendship, cured their bodies of disability and disease, and assured them of God's lasting peace. That is what St. John meant when, in the prologue of his Gospel, he said, "though the Law was given through Moses, grace and truth come through Jesus Christ." Why? Because Christ is the only-begotten Son of God who became flesh, and not only lived but, in the Eucharist, continues to live among us.

In order to draw on these resources of infinite wisdom and power, available in the Eucharist, we must believe. In the words of the *Adoro Te*, we can say: "I believe everything that the Son of God has said, and nothing can be truer than this word of the Truth. Only the Godhead was hidden on the cross, but here the humanity is hidden as well. Yet I believe and acknowledge them both."

Marian Catechists who can thus speak to Christ in the Eucharist will learn from experience what the Church means when she tells us that the Real Presence is a Sacrament. It is the same Savior who assumed our human nature to die for us on Calvary, and who now dispenses through that same humanity, now glorified, the blessing of salvation.

MARY, THE MODEL CATECHIST

20. We do not usually speak of Mary as catechist. And we do not commonly think of her as an example for those who catechize. But the Blessed Virgin is not only a pattern; she is the perfect model of what every catechist in the Catholic Church should be. (Cf. *CCC 2030*)

Before we go more deeply into our subject it may be well to ask ourselves, "What is a catechist?" A catechist is one who instructs others in the one true faith. Notice we say *instructs others*. This means teaching them by enlightening the mind, in order to inspire the will *in the one true faith*. There are many faiths. Every religion demands faith of its followers. But there is only one faith that contains the fullness of the truth. This is the faith of the Roman Catholic Church, founded by Jesus Christ.

We say that Mary is the perfect model of what every Catholic catechist should be. In saying this, we affirm what may not be obvious: that Mary was a catechist. She instructed others in the one true faith. And she did this so admirably that we may legitimately call her the Mother of Catechists.

This brings us to the fundamental question we should ask. How is Mary the perfect catechist? How can we, who are trying to instruct others in the Catholic religion, learn from her? The answer is simple. What were the main qualities of the Blessed Virgin that, as Marian Catechists, we should try to imitate? Then by following the example of Mary, we shall become more like her, who was the perfect communicator of the revelation of her divine Son.

We may identify these qualities as mainly the following:

- Mary's clear and unquestioning faith,

- Mary's union in prayer with the Heart of her Son,

- Mary's plain and courageous living out of the will of God in her life.

Given these qualities in the Blessed Virgin, we have the bedrock of Mary's qualifications as model of catechists. Why? Because the essence of catechesis is not in what is said, but in what is communicated. In order to communicate the truth a person must have a clear faith, a deep union with God in prayer, and a courageous living in conformity with the will of God.

THE FAITH OF MARY

21. To speak of Mary as model catechist, we begin where her spiritual life began: in her deep and unquestioning faith.

Faith, we know, is the acceptance by the mind of what God reveals. It means believing without a shadow of a doubt in everything which God tells us is true. Why? Because God can neither deceive nor be deceived. (Cf. *CCC 156*)

Mary had this kind of faith. At the Annunciation she believed what the angel told her, that the child she was to conceive would be the Son of the Most High.

Here was a prudent faith. After she asked, "How will this be," since she had consecrated her virginity to God, the angel assured her that the Holy Spirit would make the humanly impossible, possible. She believed.

Knowing her Scriptures, and what the prophets foretold about the sufferings of the Messiah, Mary had no illusion about what being the Messiah's mother would cost her. But she did not hesitate. She told the angel, "Be it done to me according to your word." That preposition "to" is crucial. True faith is ready to believe not only in God or in what He can do for us. It is also willing to believe in God no matter what He does to us. To see God's love in the trials of life is the proof of a clear and understanding faith. (Cf. *CCC 494*)

Faced with the dilemma that her being with child placed her in, and seeing the struggle of Joseph who knew she was innocent, Mary's faith did not weaken. She remained silent under the humiliation, until God worked the miracle of sending an angel to Joseph to accept Mary as his espoused wife.

Mary's faith sustained her through the years at Nazareth. But it was especially her faith from Calvary to Easter Sunday that the Church commemorates each Saturday of the year as a Day of Faith. She had no doubt that her Son, though crucified, would rise from the dead. (Cf. *CCC 149*)

22. There is nothing more fundamental for a catechist, nothing more needed than a share in Mary's clear and understanding faith.

Faith alone teaches. Unbelief does not. Faith alone inspires. Unbelief does not. Faith alone is used by God to communicate the faith to others. Unbelief, no matter how learned or erudite, cannot give others what it does not have. (Cf. *GDC, 141*)

Academic knowledge is useful. Faith is indispensable. Pedagogy is an asset, provided it is built on faith. But without faith, pedagogy is not only a liability, it is a seduction. (Cf. *GDC, 141*)

Like Mary, a catechist teaches almost without catechizing. Certainly our Lady did not give classes, and the number of her spoken words recorded in the Gospels is small, very small. Yet St. Augustine does not hesitate calling Mary "a living catechism," because that is what she was. She taught by living what she believed.

Marian Catechists will also teach only in so far as, like Mary, they live out what they believe.

THE PRAYER OF MARY

23. The Blessed Virgin prayed. Tradition tells us she was at prayer when the Archangel Gabriel appeared to her to tell her she was chosen to be the Mother of God. (Cf. *CCC 2617*)

At the Visitation, she prayed the Magnificat. At Bethlehem, there is not a single word of conversation with other people, related of Mary. There is only one sentence. After the shepherds had seen the Infant Jesus and proceeded to tell everyone about their marvelous experience, the evangelist simply says, "But Mary kept in mind all these things, pondering them in her heart." (Luke 2:19) Mary's prayer was prayer of the heart. In a word, Mary prayed in the depths of her being, uniting herself with Jesus, who she knew was at once her Creator and her Child.

Again at the Presentation, not a single word quoting Mary in conversation with the priest in the Temple, or with Simeon or Anna. Simeon spoke to Mary, but we are not told whether or what she spoke with him. She was, we are sure, wrapped in prayer.

Once more, at the Finding in the Temple, when Joseph and Mary found Jesus, His mother asked Him why He had done what He did. His answer was that He had to be about His real heavenly Father's business. So for the second time, St. Luke tells us that, "His mother kept all these things carefully in her heart." (Luke 2:51) This is the only recorded statement of what Mary did during the long years that she lived with her Son at Nazareth.

THE PRAYER OF A MARIAN CATECHIST

24. As with faith, so with prayer, it is impossible to really catechize unless the catechist really prays. (Cf. *CCC 153*)

Call it vocal prayer or meditation. Call it mental prayer or the liturgy. Call it aspirations or quiet moments with God. By whatever name, prayer is the lifeblood of religious instruction. And a person will only be as supernaturally successful as a catechist as the person is a man or woman of prayer.

We touch on the heart of catechesis when we say that a catechist must pray. There are many reasons for this, but especially two: Prayer is the ordinary source of grace to enlighten our minds, and prayer is the ordinary source of grace for moving our wills.

There are really two minds and two wills involved here. And both need, absolutely need, the grace that in God's ordinary providence comes only through prayer. (Cf. *CCC, 155*)

a) There is, first of all, the mind of the catechist. Rote knowledge of the Church's teaching or even the most extensive study of theology cannot, of itself, give that personal awareness of revealed truth which only divine grace can provide. "Lord, that I may see," should be the prayer of every Marian Catechist who is serious about sharing one's own deeply interior insights into God's revelation.

b) Not only is prayer necessary to know the meaning of what, as a catechist, I am teaching. Prayer is also needed to know how I am to teach it. Adaptation to different ages and abilities is assured. But this is more. Only God who reads the hearts of people knows how best I can teach and reach their hearts. And He will tell me, on one condition, that I have the wisdom to ask Him to enlighten me.

c) As a catechist, I also need to have my will inspired by God's grace, so He can use me as His channel to inspire others as I teach. There is such a thing as wanting to teach others the faith. This is not only a willingness to instruct others. It is the deep desire to bring others closer to God by what I teach them. But I will have this desire only in the measure that I am a person who prays.

There is such a thing as being a teacher without being an apostle. Whereas every true catechist should be an apostolic teacher. A catechist has a sense of mission, as one who is sent by Christ, not unlike the first Apostles who were sent by the Master to give others a share of the truth which they had first received from Him. Catechesis is not an employment, it is not a job, it is not even in the popular sense of the word, a profession. Catechesis is an apostolate. (Cf. *GDC 239*)

But that is only half the reason why Marian Catechists must pray to obtain grace for themselves. Those whom they catechize must also receive grace. Here too the prayer of the catechist is a reservoir of grace for those who are being catechized.

They need grace to grasp what they are being taught. It must "make sense" to them. They must be clear in seeing what their faith is telling them, and absolutely certain that what they are told to believe is true. They must be able to defend the truth they receive, although persons all around them either do not believe, or do not believe as firmly, or may even persecute the believers for holding on to what some educated people say is outmoded, or pre-conciliar, or out of touch with the times.

To believe in this way, they need all the light they can receive from God. And the catechist will obtain this light for them, provided the catechist prays. (Cf. *CCC 2621*)

Moreover, those who are being catechized also need superhuman strength for their wills. The mysteries of the faith, we say, are naturally inconceivable to human reason. True. But they are also naturally impossible to the naked human will.

Without an abundance of supernatural grace, to be obtained through prayer, the beautiful truths of the faith will remain just that, beautiful ideals to admire. If these truths are to be put into practice, not once or occasionally but a lifetime, a lifetime of divine help is required.

The principal font of this divine assistance is the grace of God. And the principal way to obtain this grace is by prayer, here the prayer of the catechists for those under their care.

THE LIFE OF MARY

25. If we were to describe the life of Mary in one sentence, we could say that Mary lived in constant conformity with the will of God.

We return to the Annunciation. There it was the will of God that Mary submit her will to His. She did.

The angel did not tell her to go to visit her kinswoman Elizabeth. At most he intimated she might do so. She recognized what we may call, "the implied" will of God. She acted on the inspiration immediately. The evangelist even says she did so "with haste." The least "divine suggestion," and she was off to do it.

Mary's Magnificat is a library of information of what it means to do the will of God:

- To do the will of God is to magnify the Lord, that is to praise Him, and not to look for praise or recognition for oneself.

- To do the will of God is to rejoice in God's will, no matter how naturally reluctant we may be.

- To do God's will is to see myself as lowly, no matter what great things God may do through me.

- To do God's will is to fear the Lord, not as a cowering slave but as one who fears to offend the one we love.

- To do God's will is not to aspire to earthly power or riches but to be satisfied with little and to be willing to be poor.

In a word, to do God's will is to see one-self as a mere servant who claims no rights from God but is always conscious of the duties that a servant should fulfill.

As she stood beneath the cross, Mary knew it was God's will that she be there, suffering in spirit in union with her Son.

And after His Ascension, Mary also knew it was the divine will that she be with the Apostles and disciples to wait for the coming of the Holy Spirit.

Always she saw the will of God as the Providence of God in her life. She saw the circumstances in which she found herself as part of His all-wise plan in her regard. And she responded accordingly. Always she saw the mysterious hand of God in the actions of human beings, including Augustus Caesar who ordered the census that forced her to go to Bethlehem to give birth to her Child, including Herod who forced her to flee to Egypt with the same Child in her arms, and including Pilate who condemned her Son and the executioners who nailed Him to the cross.

THE LIFE OF A MARIAN CATECHIST

26. Our spiritual life is the principal textbook from which we are to instruct others in the Catholic faith. (Cf. *GDC 239*)

This is where Mary is more than just a role model for us catechists to imitate. She is, in the deepest sense, our divinely chosen guide.

Remember that Mary, unlike her divine Son, had to believe and hope in God. Her spiritual life, therefore, was based on the same two fundamental virtues that other catechists must possess. In the measure in which our lives are built on the faith and trust that Mary had, God will use us not only to catechize but to evangelize and even convert souls to Himself beyond our fondest dreams.

THE VICAR OF CHRIST

27. The purpose of the Marian Catechists, as stated in the opening words of the manual, includes cultivating a special loyalty to the Vicar of Christ, the Bishop of Rome.

In order to appreciate what this means, it will be useful to recall the divine intervention which inspired St. Ignatius of Loyola to place himself and his first companions at the disposal of the Pope. It was in November 1537 that Ignatius had a vision of the Eternal Father, associated with His Son, who told Ignatius, "I will be favorable to you in Rome." This vision at La Storta (near Rome) fixed irrevocably in Ignatius' mind the decision to be in the service of Christ in the person of His Vicar, the Roman Pontiff.

The core of this decision was "service." He wished to serve Christ the King and so placed himself at the service of Christ's Vicar, the Bishop of Rome. He would be at the Pope's disposal wherever the Pontiff might want his (and his companions') service, especially for the teaching of Christian doctrine.

In this idea of servant also lies the special vow that Ignatius required of the professed members of his order. They are to be at the complete disposal of the Vicar of Christ, for any service whatsoever.

Papal Primacy

28. Marian Catechists are to understand the meaning of the papal primacy and its practical implications. They should be able to explain this fundamental doctrine to those whom they teach. (Cf. *CIC*, canon 330-331)

Literally "first in rank," as applied to the Pope it is a primacy not merely of honor but of jurisdiction. The Bishop of Rome has full and supreme teaching, legislative, and priestly powers in the Catholic Church.

St. Peter was promised the primacy when Christ told him he was to be the rock on which the Savior would build His Church. (Matthew 16:18) Peter actually received the primacy when the risen Christ told him to "feed my lambs, tend my sheep, feed my sheep." The feeding was to be the nourishment of the minds of the faithful with Christ's revealed truth. The tending of the sheep was to be the guidance of the wills. Even the word "lambs," placed first by Christ in His triple commission to Peter is significant. The Pope's first responsibility is to nourish the youngest members of Christ's flock, the children, with the truth that leads to eternal life. (Cf. *CCC 881*)

It therefore follows from the dogma of the primacy that even St. Paul, like the other Apostles, was subordinate to Peter as the supreme head of the whole Church.

According to Christ's ordinance, Peter was to have successors in his primacy over the entire Church and for all time.

As defined by the First Vatican Council, it is an article of faith that, "in virtue of the decree of Our Lord Jesus Christ Himself, blessed Peter has perpetual successors in his primacy over the universal Church." (July 18, 1870)

The Second Vatican Council reaffirmed "this teaching concerning the institution, the permanence, the nature and import of the sacred primacy of the Roman Pontiff and his infallible teaching office." Moreover, it went on to declare that "the body of bishops" in the Catholic Church "has no authority unless united with the Roman Pontiff, Peter's successor as its head." Indeed, "the Roman Pontiff, by reason of his office as Vicar of Christ, namely, and as pastor of the entire Church, has full, supreme, and universal power over the whole Church, a power which he can always exercise unhindered." (Second Vatican Council, Dogmatic Constitution on the Church, *Lumen Gentium (LG),* 21 November 1964, 18, 22)

Practical Implications

29. The foregoing doctrine on the papal primacy has some very practical implications for Marian Catechists.

a. Daily prayers for the Holy Father are recommended. One prayer, among others, is the Collect of the Mass for the Roman Pontiff: "O God, who in the counsel of Your providence, have built Your Church upon blessed Peter, to be the head of the other Apostles, mercifully look on our Pope _____, and grant that the one whom You have made Peter's successor, may be for Your people the visible principle and foundation of their unity of faith and communion. Through our Lord Jesus Christ, Your Son, who lives and reigns with You and the Holy Spirit, one God, forever and ever. Amen."

b. Recite the Morning Offering, which should close with the words "and in particular for the intentions of the Holy Father." Then specify the Holy Father's intentions for the month, as provided by the national office of the Apostleship of Prayer.

c. Become familiar with the history of the Popes. It shows the superhuman providence of God in preserving this divine institution over the centuries. The monumental forty-volume *History of the Popes* by Ludwig von Pastor is only a fraction of the available literature which proves that the papacy is "the most ancient and still most vigorous of dynasties."

d. Begin to accumulate, for ready reference, the most important among the hundreds of papal documents dealing with every important phase of Catholic doctrine on faith and morals.

e. Keep in touch with the statements and decisions of the Pope and the Holy See through such publications as the English weekly edition of *L'Osservatore Romano.*

f. Memorize the names and dates of the most prominent papal declarations of the Vicar of Christ in the Church's history.

g. Keep a file of ready quotations from the Popes, especially from the reigning Pontiff.

h. As a catechist, make use of your knowledge of papal history and teaching to illustrate and verify what you are teaching.

Three papal documents should be normative for Marian Catechists, namely:

- *On Evangelization in the Modern World* (*Evangelii Nuntiandi*) by Pope Paul VI. Published in 1975, it sets down the basic principles and directives for proclaiming the Gospel to the people of today. The focus is on the need for evangelizing those who have not yet received the Gospel, re-evangelizing those who have lost their faith commitment, and strengthening the Catholic religion among those who are living in a secularist or even atheistic society.

- *On Catechesis in Our Time (Catechesi Tradendae)* by Pope John Paul II. Issued in 1979, it builds on the preceding document of Pope Paul VI. Its purpose is to spell out in great detail how the true faith should be taught to every segment of society, but especially to those who have been baptized. It may be considered the single most basic document that Marian catechists are, prayerfully, to study and faithfully put into practice.

- *The Role of the Christian Family in the Modern World (Familiaris Consortio)* also by Pope John Paul II. One of the longest apostolic exhortations in papal history, it was released in 1981 to meet three grave needs that affect family life in our day: 1) moral support for those "who are already aware of the value of marriage and the family and seek to live it faithfully," 2) enlightenment for those "who are uncertain and anxious and searching for the truth" and 3) assistance to those "who are unjustly impeded from living freely their family lives." On all three levels, *Familiaris Consortio* is an indispensable guide for Marian Catechists, particularly in training parents to provide sound religious instruction for their children.

Scope of the Marian Catechist Apostolate

30. Consistent with the foregoing pontifical documents, there are five levels of apostolic zeal for the Marian Catechists.

Infants

31. Pope John Paul II declared, it is "decisive" that "the very young child receives the first elements of catechesis from its parents and the family surroundings." He

further said, "I cannot insist too strongly on the early initiation by Christian parents in which the child's faculties are integrated into a living relationship with God. It is a work of prime importance." (*CT* 36)

It is therefore a primary responsibility of Marian Catechists to encourage and help train parents for this important task.

There is more at stake here than the obvious fact that the earliest impressions of infancy have the deepest influence on our human faculties. At Baptism, the infant receives the infused virtues of faith, hope and charity. These virtues enable the mind and will to know, desire and love far beyond their natural capacity. But in God's ordinary providence, these supernatural powers must be nurtured from the moment they are received.

32. As the infant enters childhood, it is again not only the child's natural powers of intelligence and volition that need to be developed. It is also, and with emphasis, the supernatural gifts that were received at Baptism.

That is why the Popes stress the need for "a catechesis aimed at inserting him or her organically into the life of the Church," including preparation for the sacraments.

Also stressed is the quality of this catechesis. It should be "didactic in character" yet "directed towards giving witness to the faith." Moreover, even in childhood, the religious instruction though initial, should not be fragmentary. It is to "reveal, although in an elementary way, all the principal mysteries of the faith and their effects on the child's moral and religious life." Especially crucial is the need for teaching children the "meaning of the sacraments," while providing them with the supernatural experience that comes from receiving the sacraments. (Cf. *GDC 178*)

ADOLESCENTS

33. As children reach puberty and adolescence, their religious education should take into account the following aspects of their lives (Cf. *GDC 185*):

- the discovery of their own personality;
- the time for making plans for the future;
- the rise of noble impulses of generosity;
- an awakened feeling of love;
- the desire to be with other people;
- the experience of internal joy at the exhilarating discovery of life.

But adolescents must also be taught how to cope with certain problems that come at this stage of their development:

- the biological impulses of sexuality;
- the strong desire to understand what they believe;
- the corresponding impulse to question what, as children, they simply took for granted;
- the frustration, sometimes bordering on anguish, at not knowing the reason for what they are told to do or avoid;
- a tendency to dangerous introspection;
- a corresponding tendency to mistrust others, including their parents and those in authority;
- the first experiences of disappointment at not measuring up to expectations, or not being accepted by their peers;
- the first experience of failure, either real or imaginary.

Centuries of the Church's wisdom has shown how much adolescents need to learn all they can about Jesus Christ. Their religious education must be strongly Christocentric. They must find in Christ "a Friend, Guide and Model, whom they can not only admire but imitate." They should see in Him the only Person who can solve the problems of a suffering humanity, and the only one with whom they can identify as they begin to struggle with their own difficulties and fears.

YOUNG ADULTS

34. In teaching religion to young adults, the Church urges catechists to be open and practical in presenting the truths of faith.

More than any persons their age in previous history, young adults are living in a world that has become a global village. Issues like international peace and the advancement of human dignity, development of nations and liberation from economic slavery, social justice and concern for the poor are on the minds of the young. These issues need the solid ground of Catholic faith and moral principles, which the catechist should provide.

The youth should also be helped to make lifetime decisions, whether to marry or stay single, and if single, whether to remain celibate in the world or go on for the priesthood or a consecrated life in a religious or secular institute or other form of consecrated life. (Cf. *GDC 184*)

ADULTS

35. There are two aspects of religious instruction of adults that specially concern the Church in modern times. They may be called the problem of de-christianization and the need for training lay catechists.

Pope Paul VI spoke of the widespread "de-christianization in our day." (Paul VI, Apostolic Exhortation, *Evangelii Nuntiandi [EN]*, 8 December 1975, 52) As a result, millions of baptized Catholics should be catechized or, as Pope John Paul II said, "re-evangelized."Three types of such nominal Catholic adults need religious instruction:

- Persons who were born in sociologically Christian surroundings but have never been educated in their faith;

- Persons who had received some religious education in early life but the education was badly imparted or badly assimilated;

- Persons who had been duly instructed but later drifted away from all religious practice.

Lay catechists are a providential answer to the desperate need for religious instruction in the Catholic faith. This applies to both evangelization of non-Christian people and catechesis for the baptized.

Africa is a dramatic example of what lay catechists can do. As missionary societies were being formed at the turn of the last century, they trained the faithful among the laity to spread the Gospel among the natives. The results were astounding.

We have the official statistics for two years, that were light years apart. In 1906 there were 360,000 Catholics in Africa, for a total population of 130 million. In 1986 there were 75 million Catholics for a total population of 572 million in all the countries of Africa. This represents a growth of some 4000 percent, which has no parallel in recorded Catholic missionary history. Historians of the continent attribute this phenomenal development of Catholic Christianity mainly to the organized and dedicated zeal of lay catechists.

It is becoming increasingly clear that what was done in Africa needs to be done in other continents. Pope John Paul II paid a tribute to lay catechists for their apostolic achievement in the past, and expressed his prayerful hopes for the future.

I am anxious to give thanks in the Church's name to all of you, lay teachers of catechesis in the parishes, the men and the still more numerous women throughout the world, who are devoting yourselves to the religious education of many generations. Your work is often lowly and hidden but it is carried out with ardent and generous zeal, and it is an eminent form of the lay apostolate, a form that is particularly important where for various reasons children and young people do not receive suitable religious training in the home.

But the term "catechists" belongs above all to the catechists in mission lands. Born of families that are already Christian or converted at some time to Christianity and instructed by missionaries or by another catechist, they consecrate their lives, year after year, to catechizing children and adults in their own country. Churches that are flourishing today would not have been built up without them. I rejoice at the efforts made by the Sacred Congregation for the Evangelization of Peoples to improve more and more the training of these catechists. I gratefully recall the memory of those whom the Lord has already called to Himself. I beg the intercession of those whom my predecessors have raised to the glory of the altars. I express the wish that many others may succeed them and that

they may increase in numbers for a
task so necessary for the missions.
(*CT* 66)

Marian Catechists should often reflect on
these words of the Holy Father. Their
apostolate will certainly be among believing
Catholics; but it will also be to people who
need to be re-evangelized and in once Christian countries that are literally becoming
"mission lands." (Cf. *ChL 34)*

WAYS AND MEANS TO BE
USED BY MARIAN CATECHISTS

36. As a general principle, Marian Catechists
    are to use every available means of pro-
    claiming and explaining Christ and His
    Church. Pope John Paul II identified
    these means as the following:

- Oral communication, to individual persons or groups;

- The media of social communication, namely television, radio, books, periodicals and newspapers and the whole range of audio-visual recordings.

The Second Vatican Council was the first general council of the Church since the dawn of the communications age. Marian Catechists are to become totally familiar with the Council's teaching as found in the Decree on the Means of Social Communication, for example:

> The Catholic Church was founded by Christ our Lord to bring salvation to all men. She believes that her task involves employing the means of social communication to pronounce the good news of salvation.

> It will be principally for the laity to animate these media. [To this end] lay people must be given the necessary

technical, doctrinal and moral formation. (Second Vatican Council, Decree
on the Means of Social Communication, *Inter Mirifica [IM]*, 4 December
1963, 3, 15)

In the light of this conciliar teaching,
Marian Catechists are to consider the use of
the media as a grave responsibility to pro-
mote the Kingdom of Christ to the farthest
reaches of the earth. (Cf. *GDC 161)*

Family Catechists

37. This will be one of the longest sections of
the manual. The reason is that the future
of the Catholic Church in any part of the
world depends mainly on the parents'
awareness of their rights and responsibilities in the religious education of their
children. (Cf. *CIC* 226)

Whatever else Marian Catechists do, the
first priority of their apostolate is to instruct

and motivate Catholic parents to nurture the faith and moral values of the children whom they have physically brought into the world. It is essential that the children receive sound orthodox Catholic teaching. A focus of the Marian Catechists should be on young parents with children and on home education, that is, those parents who are educating their children in their homes.

We shall speak of rights *and* responsibilities. A word of explanation of these two terms is called for.

A right is the moral claim that a person has to possess something or to do something which others have the duty to respect.

Rights therefore correspond to duties. For example, we have a right to our reputation; other people have the duty to respect it and not do it injury. That would be an injustice.

A responsibility, on the other hand, is different. It is the moral obligation which follows from some position or office that we receive or assume. A responsibility always pertains, for our purpose, to some other person or persons who, then, depend upon us. They, in turn, have a right to expect us to fulfill our responsibility.

The focus of this section of the manual is to cover both aspects of the subject, but separately. First to speak of the rights, and then of the responsibilities.

Concerning parental rights in religious education we shall see:

- what these rights are, concretely and specifically;

- from whom these rights do not derive;

- from whom these rights do derive.

Then we shall ask how parents are to satisfy their moral obligations. Finally, we shall briefly say something about the role of Marian Catechists in assisting parents to fulfill their responsibilities to the children whom God has given them.

WHAT ARE PARENTAL RIGHTS?

38. Stated concisely: Parents have the right to give their offspring a share in their own life of the spirit, corresponding to the share they have given them in their life of the body. Or, in more concrete terms, parents have the right to communicate their own religious beliefs and practices to the sons and daughters to whom they have already communicated their physical existence as human beings.

We have closely identified the rights of the father and mother to rear their family spiritually with their natural rights to bring the family physically into being.

This is not coincidental. The one follows the other. No less than a married couple has a natural right to beget children, who are like the parents as human persons; so a married couple has the corresponding right to procreate children who are like their parents as religious persons.

From Whom Do Parental Rights Not Derive? There are several reasons why this question should be asked, namely:

- because a growing state monopoly in education is implying the contrary;

- because vested interests, and not all secular, are practically claiming the opposite;

- because some philosophers of education are urging positions different from the one commonly held by historic Catholicism.

From whom, then, do parents' rights in education, and especially religious education, not derive?

They do not derive from the state or from civil society. Not only does the Church teach this, but, to its credit, the U. S. Supreme Court in the famous Oregon Case (1925) ruled that an Oregon state law requiring all children to attend public schools was unconstitutional. Pope Pius XI favorably cited this judicial decision in his famous encyclical *Christian Education of Youth* (1929). The court stated:

> As often heretofore pointed out, rights guaranteed by the Constitution may not be abridged by legislation which has no reasonable relation to some purposes within the competence of the state.

The fundamental theory of liberty upon which all governments in the Union repose excludes any general power of the state to standardize its children by forcing them to accept instruction from public teachers only.

The child is not the mere creature of the state. Those who nurture him and direct his destiny have the right, coupled with the high duty, to recognize and prepare him for additional obligations.

It is the denial of this position, which is one of the least publicized but most agonizing features of Marxist tyranny, where the state claims prior rights over the parents to educate the child (from infancy) in its own materialistic ideology.

Besides not deriving from the state, parents' rights to give their children the religious education of their choice does not come from any vested interests, whether secular (which we should expect) or professedly ecclesiastical. Even the Church, while urging and encouraging parents to give their children a Catholic education, is not precisely the source of the parents' rights to confer this education. (Cf. *CIC* 1136)

- Moreover, the parents are not their own source of these rights to give their children a religious upbringing,

- as though they have an option to give them such training or not,

- or as though they may be indifferent about the kind of religious rearing the children receive.

Sources of Parental Rights

39. Twenty centuries of the Church's history tell us that the rights of fathers and mothers to give their offspring adequate and,

as far as possible, accurate religious education come from God.

Why so? Because it was He who created the human spirit and infused it into the body prepared for infusion by the mother and father. As so many childless couples sadly know, it is finally up to God whether they will have children or not.

Why so? Because God makes each immortal soul out of nothing and unites it with a body to produce a human person. This person is to serve God on earth, for which he or she needs training from infancy. Then, if they serve God faithfully in this life, they will possess the vision and happiness of God in the life to come.

PARENTAL RESPONSIBILITIES

40. Since God has given parents the privilege of bringing children into the world both physically and spiritually, He also places

on them the obligation to nurture the lives which they freely procreated.

And the duty of religious nurture is no less; in fact, it is more grave than the duty of physical nurture.

Why grave? Because none of us can either bring ourselves into existence (which is obvious), nor can any of us keep ourselves or develop in existence (which may be less obvious) by ourselves. We need help: constant, lifelong, abiding, perduring assistance from others. (Cf. *CCC* 2223)

Personal Responsibility

41. Parents are to cooperate with each other, father with mother, and not mother alone; and less still mother in one direction and father in another direction. (Cf. *CCC* 2205)

This cooperation also presumes mutual understanding of their respective roles in the religious and moral rearing of the child. Behind such mutual understanding is mutual reflection and discussion between husband and wife on how they can best contribute, each according to his and her ability, to the well-being of the offspring given to them by God.

As we get more specific about the parents' cooperative responsibility, we should identify the three ways that the parents, personally, nurture their children in things of the spirit. They do so:

- by what they are,
- by what they do,
- and by what they say.

First of all, by what they are:

What are we saying? We are saying that the most elemental means at the parents' disposal for training their children in the ways of God is by themselves living the ways of God. (Cf. *CCC 2225*)

The proverbs of all nations are filled with eloquence on the persuasive power of good example. Among dozens we could quote, there is one which says that "Example is the school of mankind, and they will learn at no other."

Yet there is more than example implied in the statement that parents best teach religion by what they are. We are here dealing in the realm of grace. In the ordinary course of providence, God uses as His instruments those who are personally most united to Him by their virtue, who are most humble and patient and pure and prayerful.

Secondly, by what they do:

This may seem to be unnecessary after having said that father and mother give religious upbringing by what they are.

On the contrary. In things of the spirit, it is not enough to be (for our purposes) a Christian and a Catholic. A person must act like one.

Why is this important to stress? Because there is in all of us a tendency to divide our lives into two compartments. There is the temptation to claim (honestly and sincerely) to be one thing and yet to behave like something else.

This moral separation in us is neither rare nor surprising. Remember St. Paul's confession about himself, "For I do not the good that I wish, but the evil that I do not wish, that I perform." (Romans 7:19)

Thirdly, by what they say:

Again we enter a region of mystery; the mystery of how our words are a channel of ourselves.

Yet we know that among all the means of self-communication, none is more universal or more effective than the spoken word.

Certainly parents can exercise their religious responsibilities through other persons and agencies.

However, what needs strong emphasis is that these other persons or agencies are auxiliary; they are not fundamental. They are secondary, not primary.

The fundamental and primary communicative agent of religious belief and practice is the parent. This is the common verdict of Christian history, as it is also the common teaching of the Catholic Church.

If we further ask, how do the parents exercise this role, there are many possible answers, but we will concentrate on just one; one that is central to religious pedagogy. It responds to that instructive sign of human intelligence which a child begins to reveal at a very early age, earlier than most people suspect. (Cf. *CCC 2227*)

Children begin to ask intelligent "why's" long before they are able to conceptualize and much less, rationalize, the meaning of their questions. The "why's" which appear between the ages of three and seven are extremely numerous. Yet we are told that this is already the second age of "why's" in the child, implying that children can begin to ask "why" before they are three years old.

Evidently it makes all the difference in the world how a child's "why's" are answered.

- The fact that questions are asked is a law of life.

- The answers received will shape that life, as we believe, not only for time but also for eternity.

Role of the Marian Catechists

42. It is impossible to exaggerate how important it is for Marian Catechists to train

parents, especially young parents, for the religious instruction of their children and to help them in this undertaking. Marian Catechists should provide this training and assistance not only to parents whose children may attend public or parochial schools but also to home educators, those parents who are educating their children in their homes.

Pope John Paul II spells out this importance in the most impressive terms. He says that the "family's catechetical activity is . . . irreplaceable." Stressed by the Second Vatican Council, it means several things:

- "Education in the faith by the parents should begin from the children's tenderest years."

- It is being given "when the members of a family help each other to grow in the faith through the witness of their Christian lives; a witness that is often without words but which perseveres throughout a day-to-day life lived in accordance with the Gospel."

- "This catechesis is more incisive when in the course of family events (such as the reception of the sacraments, the celebration of great liturgical feasts, the birth of a child, a bereavement) care is taken to explain in the home the Christian or religious significance of these events."

- "Christian parents must strive to follow and repeat, within the setting of family life, the more methodical teaching received elsewhere."

The Vicar of Christ synthesizes family catechesis by concluding that it "accompanies and enriches all other forms of catechesis." (*CT* 68)

Marian Catechists are to be specially zealous in fostering family catechesis and assist parents in the religious instruction of their children in secularized societies. The reason is obvious. Otherwise the children will grow up, perhaps nominally Catholic, but really unbelievers at heart who have only a veneer of Christianity. The Pope's statement on this subject deserves to be memorized.

In places where anti-religious legislation endeavors to prevent education in the faith, and in places where widespread unbelief or invasive secularism makes real religious growth practically impossible, "the church of the home" remains the one place where children and young people receive an authentic catechesis. Thus there cannot be too great an effort on the part of Christian parents to prepare for this ministry of being their own children's catechists and to carry it out with tireless zeal.

Then follows one sentence of Pope John Paul II which practically identifies the main task of the Marian Catechists. "Encouragement," he says, "must be given to the individuals or institutions that, through person-to-person contacts, through meetings, and through all kinds of pedagogical means, help parents to perform their task: The service they are doing to catechesis is beyond price." (*CT 68*)

In God's providence, in the years to come, Marian Catechists hope to do great things for the extension of Christ's Kingdom on earth. But nothing they do will be of more lasting benefit to souls than assisting parents in this priceless apostolate of family catechesis.

Conduct of Marian Catechists

43. Marian Catechists are to be a positive influence on persons and parishes. They

are to be Christ-like and Mary-like. To that end, Marian Catechists will exercise prudence if they become aware of errors being made in liturgical or doctrinal practice or teaching. Christian charity precludes direct confrontation or harsh criticism. Instead Marian Catechists will identify the error and use the error as an occasion to teach the truth in charity. (Cf. *CIC* 212 §3)

It is possible that a Marian Catechist, in an excess of fervent zeal or for another reason, may behave in a manner that reflects badly on or could give scandal to the Church or to the Marian Catechists. If such a situation should arise, the Marian Catechist would first be advised orally of the behavior that needs to be modified. If the offending behavior is not changed, then a written notice of the behavior and the necessary change would be sent.

Should this written notice fail to produce the necessary change in behavior, then the person's designation as a Marian Catechist would be removed.

MARIAN ASSOCIATES

44. It is not anticipated that the number of Marian Catechists will be large. Their role in the apostolate of religious instruction is to be leaders. It is assumed that their own faith commitment will be strong, and such that they will encourage others to join with them in sharing the Gospel. It may also be that their duties at home or elsewhere may prevent them from being very actively engaged in catechetical work.

Moreover, the spiritually contemplative Marian Catechists, by supposition, concentrate on their own personal union with our Lord through prayer and sacrifice.

There may also be some faithful Catholics who want to assist the apostolate of Marian Catechists by providing regular financial or other support. However, because of time or other constraints, they would be unable to meet the requirements of an active or contemplative Marian Catechist.

For all these reasons, Marian Catechists are encouraged to involve other dedicated men and women whom we shall call Marian Associates. They will assist with the catechetical apostolate of making Jesus Christ known and loved by those for whom He died on the cross.

Given the nature of this apostolate, there is a wide scope for cooperative effort. It is assured, of course, that the Marian Catechists provide the basic directives for those who are associates.

Scripture quotations are from the Saint Joseph New Catholic Edition of the Holy Bible.